FOR RICH AND GLENDA

$\overset{\overset{||}{\#}}{99}$

Dedicated to Mark Jackling Jennings

Library of Congress Catalog Card
Number 97-62506
ISBN 0-9651144-4-9

Design: Michael Cronan
Production Design: Sandra Shuhert, John Clifford, Joseph Stitzlein
Editor: Nancy Eklund
Type in Avenir, FFScala
Printed in China

William Stout Publishers
501 Greenwich Street
San Francisco, California 94133

JIM JENNINGS ARCHITECTURE

T E N   P R O J E C T S :   T E N   Y E A R S

William Stout Publishers
San Francisco

In an article that I wrote on Jim Jennings' Oliver House, I noted with some puzzlement that Jennings has been described by more than one design journalist as "an unsentimental modernist."[†] Although he has said of his own design philosophy, "My 'religion' is a non-ornamented one," this architect's view of architecture is neither coldly pragmatic nor cynically stylistic. After nearly thirty years in the profession, Jim Jennings' passion for architecture—the process of making things—and his belief in its innate ability to effect change are still idealistic enough to verge on the romantic.

Jennings is the product of a time and place that seem, in retrospect, the ideal hatchery for an architect. He was born in Santa Barbara, California, in 1940 and spent his earliest years in wartime Los Angeles. "My first memories of L.A. are essentially pre-freeway," he says, recalling seemingly endless rows of palm trees and telephone wires and riding the Red Cars out to Venice Beach with his grandmother, who worked in the Bradbury Building downtown. That building, with its

INTRODUCTION

distinctive light well and elevator, made a strong impression on Jennings, as did the Hollywood Bowl, which he visited on school field trips, and the houses by Lloyd Wright that he glimpsed while riding to and from his Hollywood neighborhood.

This early experience of Los Angeles was balanced by the six years Jennings spent in Redlands, where he and his older brother moved with their widowed mother when he was seven. The family lived on the edge of an orange grove whose owner later taught Jennings to drive a tractor. He still remembers coming home late one evening to find orange blossoms, scattered like popcorn over the trees, their fragrance permeating the night air. "I can relate to small towns," he notes, "and to the geometries and geography of agriculture." Given the impression that this experience made on him, it is no accident that Jennings considers the requirements of the site, whether urban or rural, the most important determinant of a building's design.

Subsequent moves in his teenage years took Jennings to the coast just south of Redondo Beach (his mother remarried—at Lloyd Wright's 'Wayfarers' Chapel) and then back inland to Riverside.

Although he had spent his summers doing things like plowing an asparagus field and working in an agricultural laboratory, architecture was always—at least subliminally—in the picture. "Growing up when and where I did gave me the opportunity to see so much being built. As a kid, I was always prowling around building sites," Jennings explains. On family trips to Newport Beach, he never failed to be intrigued by a building he later knew to be Schindler's Lovell House. "It wasn't that I knew I was going to be an architect," he says, "but something about it really interested me."

For someone who grew up in the post-war boom years, and who had spent his childhood figuring out how things worked, studying engineering must have seemed a logical choice. "This was the time when the Russians had launched Sputnik, and there was a huge propaganda blitz in science," Jennings recalls. But soon after he arrived at the University of California at Berkeley Jennings realized that he was in the wrong department. "I enjoyed analyzing how things worked,

but the technical aspects, especially in the pre-calculator days, were not so interesting," he says. What did seem interesting were the architecture classes that Jennings walked by on his way to school every day. "They were doing the kinds of things that I had loved to do as a child. I had always made models of boats and airplanes, I had always had projects, and I was always drawing. I dropped all that when I started college, so architecture was a reconnection to something that was important to me."

But in spite of his early disillusionment with engineering, some of Jennings' greatest influences as a student of architecture were engineers—Auguste Perret, Pier Luigi Nervi, Felix Candela. He remains fascinated by what he refers to as the "creative engineer," or "artistic scientist," the type of designer epitomized by Buckminster Fuller, or, in some sense, Frank Lloyd Wright. "Wright's more or less constant experimentation with structures and materials, his pushing the limits of making buildings in different ways," make him another of Jennings' heroes. "It's all rooted in the act of making," he says.

Jennings' Berkeley education, in the days of William Wurster, stressed technical issues—he recalls having to design a rivet for a bridge in one class—yet students were also required to study drawing and sculpture in the art department. And although architectural theory had yet to assume the importance it has assumed in schools recently, students of Jennings' generation saw architects design structures that were quite radical for their time; Jennings feels that today, nearly the opposite is true. "Recent academic discourse has resulted in the application of conditions to architecture that don't come from making buildings," he argues. "Back then, there was more optimism, a greater willingness to consider new materials or new ways to build. There was a faith in the future that is generally lacking today."

It is this search for pushing the limits that informs Jennings' modernist predilections. "Issues of scale, proportion, how light enters and defines a space, the relationship between inside and outside—all those issues can be expressed in architecture without having to rely on traditional historical methods," he insists. Yet many of Jennings' buildings have an almost classical calm, as in the Barclay Simpson Sculpture Studio at California College of Arts and Crafts—an elegant, reductive structure consisting of a concrete base and steel structure with glass-block and cementboard panel infill—or the Oliver House, with its asymmetrical, solid volumes that encase soaring, light-filled interiors. And while Jennings' current works—most notably the Italian Cemetery project—explore the metaphysical aspects of space and circulation, structural and material innovation still provides the focus for his architectural aspirations.

Even though it was a theoretical project, Jennings' design for a one-hundred story skyscraper, commissioned for a 1991 exhibition at the San Francisco Museum of Modern Art, remains, to its designer, a retort to contemporary architecture's lack of mission. "The idea of a one-hundred story building on a residential lot intrigued me because of the commonly-held bias against tall buildings," he explains. Rather than seeing the skyscraper as a demon of modern urban life, Jennings envisions an ultra-modern, "green" structure that would be self-sustaining, making an environmental impact that would be minimal relative to the population it contained. But such a project would require

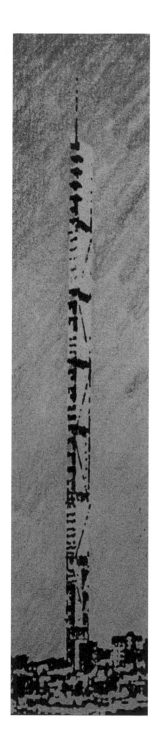

materials and building methods much more advanced than either current practice or codes support. "New technologies have been conspicuously absent from architectural thinking for the past twenty years," Jennings adds. The tall building project offered him the opportunity to investigate the current state of research into new materials and building systems. This enquiry also led to a consulting relationship with an engineering firm—the office of Ove Arup.

That the skyscraper project is for Jennings about process rather than form—despite the fact that his designs maintain a consistent formal elegance—is indicative of the kind of social idealism that is increasingly absent from architectural thinking today. "I think architects should be advocates for change and for intelligence in the way we do things," he asserts. "When people are thinking creatively, there is not much difference between art or design or science or any other activity," says Jennings. He laments the fact that there is no architectural equivalent of the space program or the America's Cup yacht race. "Both are based on performance, and design and technology get pushed to their limits. You can design a really interesting-looking sail, but if it isn't based on performance, it doesn't make any sense at all." Jennings' sails already look interesting, but if he has his way, they will carry his buildings ever more swiftly through the waters of change.

†Pilar Viladas, "San Francisco Skyline: Crisp Geometries on Telegraph Hill," *Architectural Digest* 54, no. 8 (August 1997), 80. All other information quoted in this essay is taken from a series of conversations between the author and Jim Jennings that occurred in 1996.

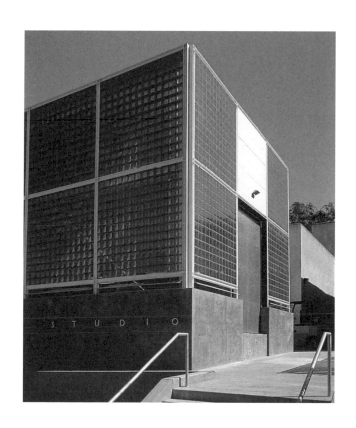

This project was designed to provide studio space for the glass and sculpture departments of the California College of Arts and Crafts, a private art college located in Oakland, California. By combining the studio space of these departments, the administration hoped to promote inter-disciplinary interaction between students in each field. The studio is housed in a single room containing a glass furnace at one end and a pair of large sliding doors at the other. A pit is formed within the concrete floor to accommodate the casting of large pieces of glass, and a gantry crane

BARCLAY SIMPSON SCULPTURE STUDIO

used for moving large works of art runs the length of the space. The building is constructed in two parts. The lower part is made from materials of the earth—sand, cement, rock, and water—that combine to form concrete. The upper part is made from materials born of fire—glass and steel. Attached to the skeletal steel framework of the building is a secondary steel frame, which holds in place large panels of glass blocks. Designed in response to aesthetic as well as functional criteria, the glass block walls allow diffused natural light to enter the interior of the building by day; when lit from within by night, the building radiates light, becoming a beacon of creative energy.

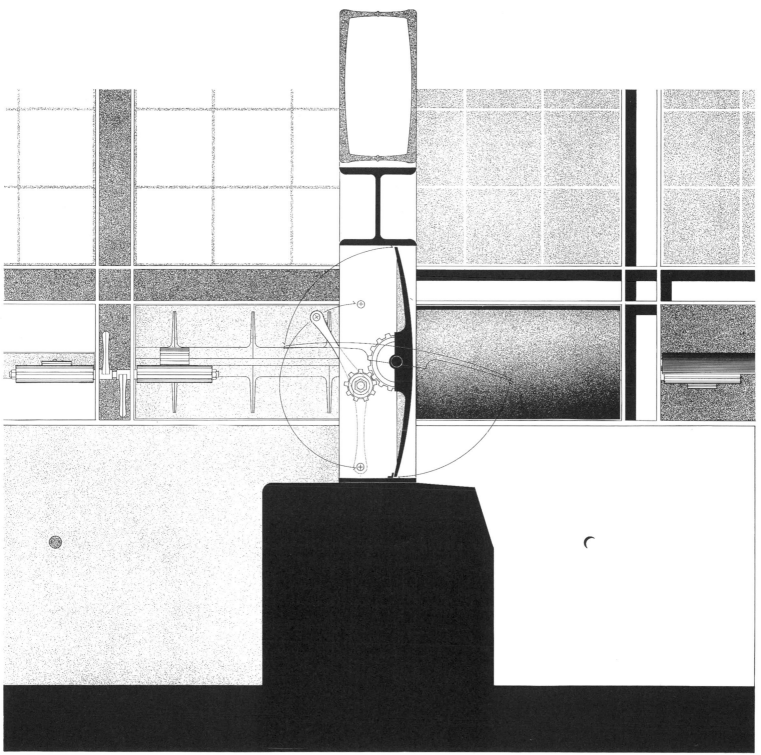

Detail of lower ventilation flap

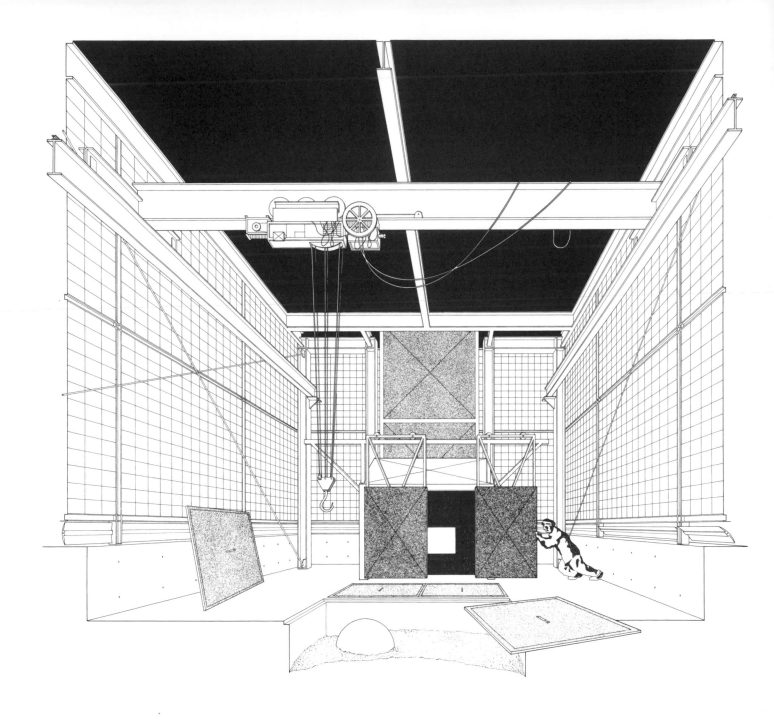

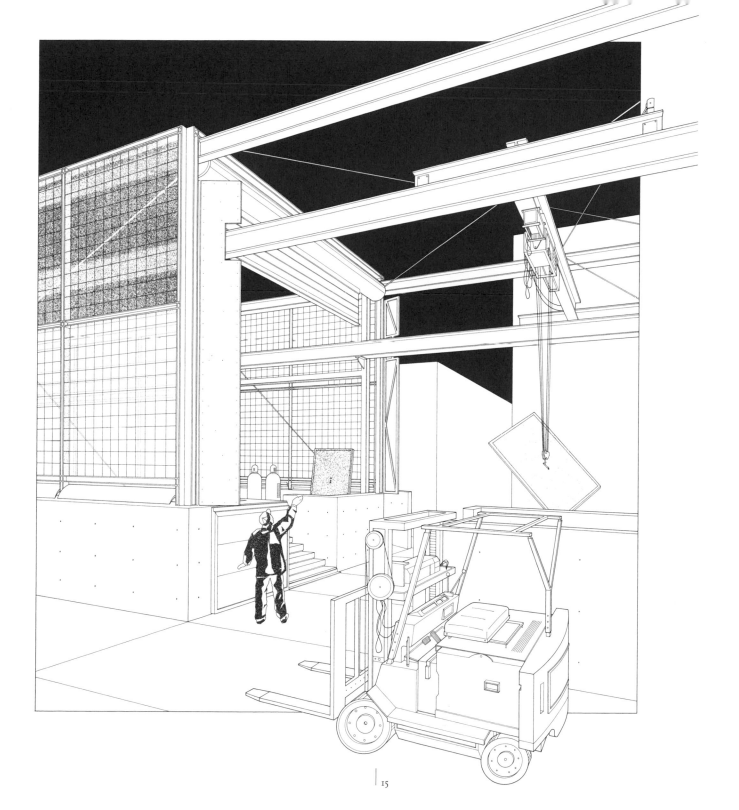

16

Tuesday, April 23, at 9:00 pm

17

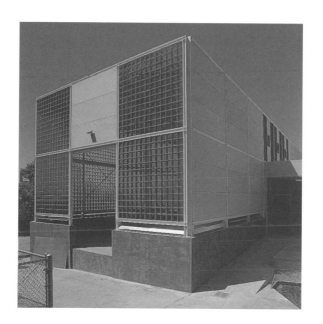

The end of the building opposite the glass furnace opens to allow for the delivery of raw materials and the removal of finished works of art. Because the entire interior space is traversed by an industrial crane, large or heavy objects can be moved at will. Materials storage and a casting "breakout" area are located in a space that links the studio with an existing building.

Passive heating and cooling devices modulate the climate within the studio. Heat generated as a by-product of the annealing process is retained within the massive concrete base of the building; solar heat gain takes place through the glass block of its upper elevations. The space is cooled through a process of natural ventilation. Manually operated flaps located near the floor allow air to enter the building freely; louvered panels placed at ceiling-level allow warm air to escape. The flow of air through the building can be increased when necessary through the use of high-powered fans located in the center of each louvered panel.

The site selected for this project is located on a sheep ranch near Geyserville, California, owned by two art collectors. Portions of the ranch have been set aside for the installation of commissioned works of outdoor sculpture. The program for this project is to provide two guest suites for visiting artists. The suites are sited on the crest of a knoll near the main house. A cut is made into the hillside, and two 200–foot long concrete walls are inserted into the cut. The guest suites occupy the space in between the walls. Submerged within the hillside, the suites are barely visible from the main house. The two suites share a central courtyard. In addition, each suite opens onto its own outdoor space through large glass panels placed at its end. Views through these glass panels to the

VISITING ARTIST SUITES

surrounding pastures, sculpture, and a small lake are framed by the concrete walls that line the sides of the cut made through the hillside. The panels pivot to allow access to the adjacent landscape, to the main house, to the artist's studios, and to other facilities located on the property. Each suite contains a sleeping room, bath, and living room. Walls, floors, and roof slabs are made of poured-in-place concrete and define the basic volumes of the building. Interior partitions, doors, and shelving are made of resin-impregnated plywood, intended to express the freestanding interior elements as pieces of large-scale furniture. Carpets laid on the polished concrete floor provide color, softness, and texture on a small scale.

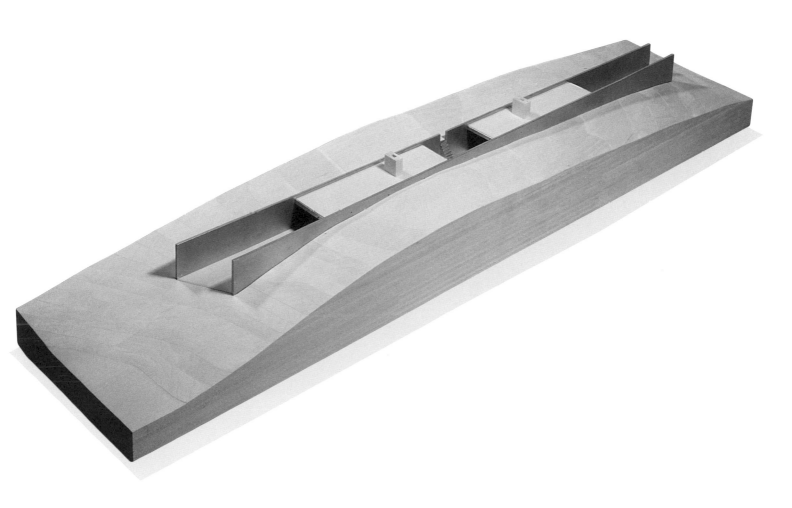

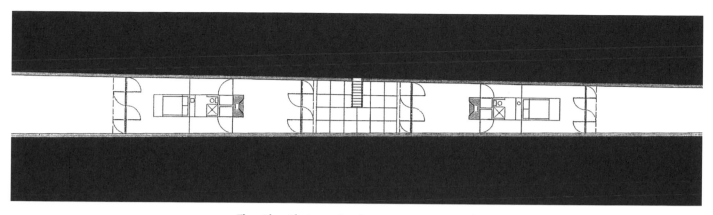

Floor Plan. The two suites share a common courtyard.

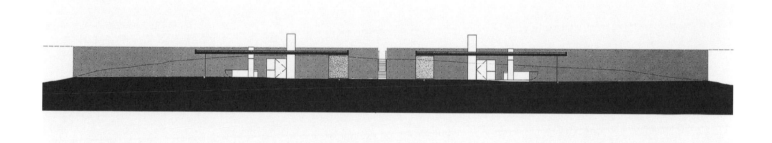

Longitudinal section. Changing floor slopes alter the spatial proportions of the suites.

Elevation. The building appears as a long, uninterrupted concrete wall, pushed into the hillside.

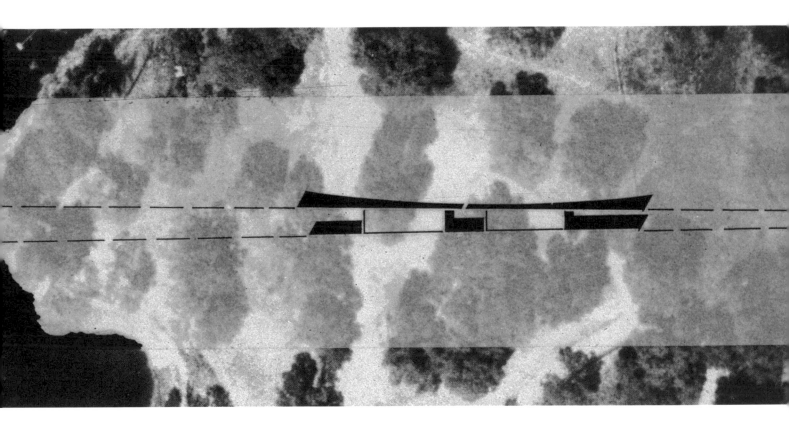

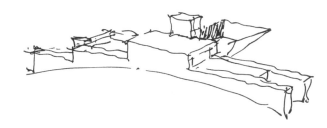

Although the walls of the house appear to be parallel, they actually are not. In one direction, the walls visually converge on a spot occupied by a piece of outdoor sculpture. In the opposite direction, they diverge toward a small lake. As a result, the building functions in effect as a "perceptual telescope."

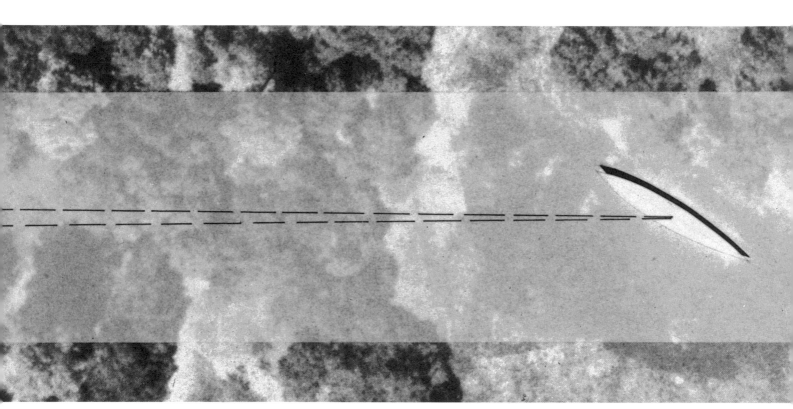

Unlike a refracting telescope, which causes distant objects viewed in the diverging direction to appear larger and nearer than they actually are, the "perceptual telescope" causes objects viewed through the converging space—in this case, the sculpture—to appear larger and closer at hand.

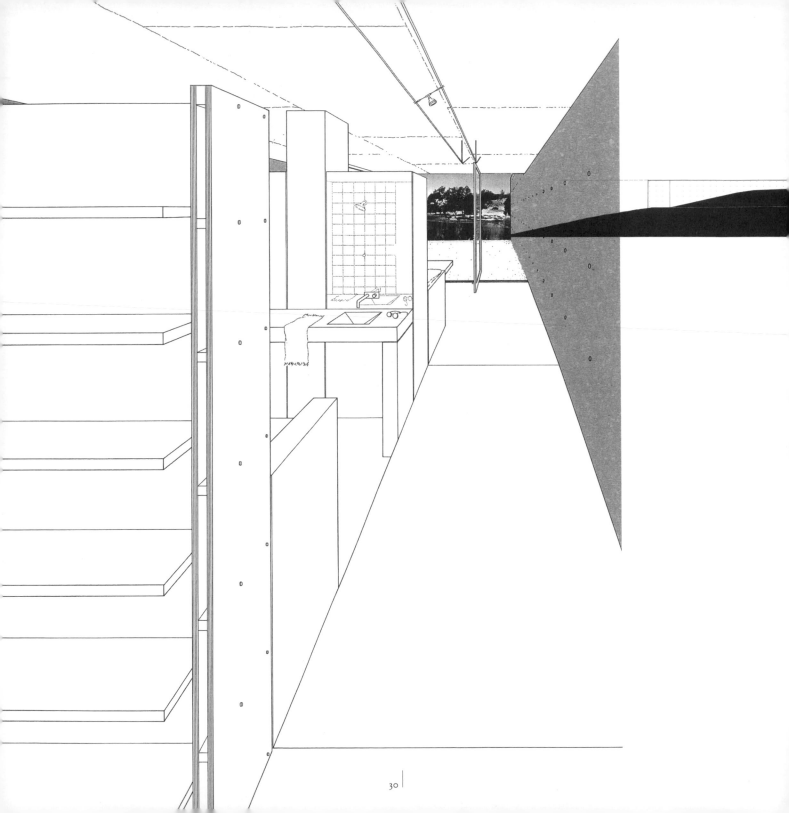

Each of the guest suites takes on a
different spatial character as the result
of changes in plan and section that occur
along the length of the building. In the
suite in which the walls converge to
frame the view of a distant sculpture, the
exterior ground plane also slopes upward.
This heightens the visual effect of con-
vergence created by the walls.

In the suite in which the walls diverge, the view opens horizontally toward a nearby lake. Here the ground plane slopes downward to accentuate the horizontal orientation of the space. This shifting of the horizontal and vertical planes throughout the building's section heightens the perspective phenomena of foreshortening and elongation.

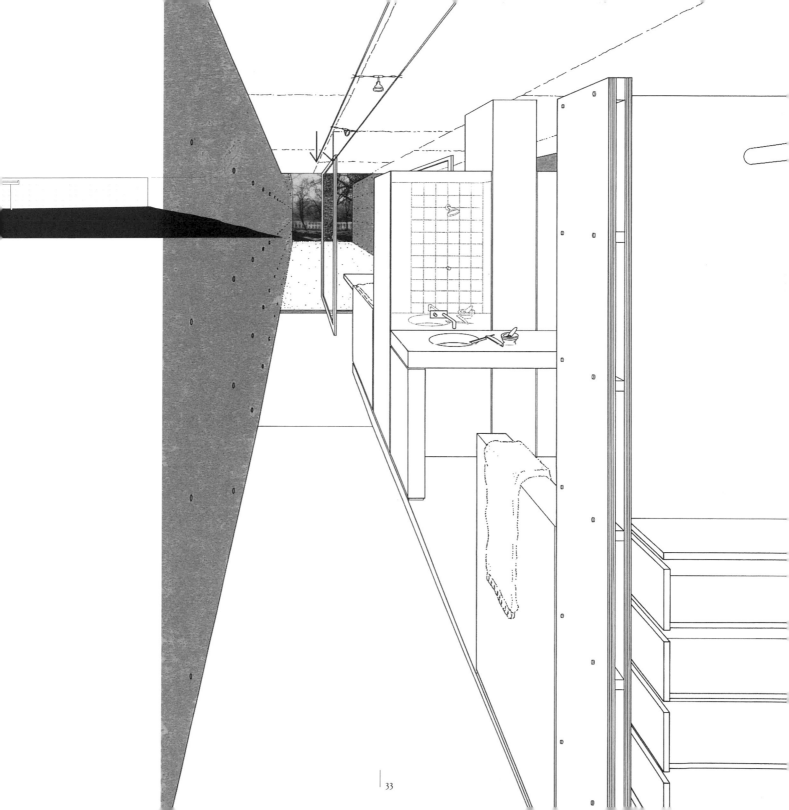

This residence is built on a site in the Oakland Hills that was cleared by the fire of 1991. The client's original home and all of its contents were destroyed in the fire. Rather than sell the property, she decided to rebuild on the site. The house is designed primarily as a response to the site—a steep, sloping hillside with panoramic views to the surrounding landscape and to the bay beyond. Burrowed into the hillside, the building is anchored to the site. A space is excavated from within the overall volume of the building to create a private, south-facing, exterior courtyard. The programmatic elements of the project are

BECKER RESIDENCE

grouped around this central courtyard within two distinct volumes. The kitchen, living areas, and a large bedroom suite are located in the volume to the east; additional bedrooms, a garage, and a storage area are located to the west. A series of bridging elements traverse the two-story central courtyard and join together the two volumes. At the upper level, a platform connects the two halves of the house, becoming an outdoor room. At the lower level, a protected, sun-filled courtyard is formed within the embrace of the building. This space constitutes the heart of the house and provides the occupants with the freedom of living with privacy both in-doors and out-of-doors simultaneously.

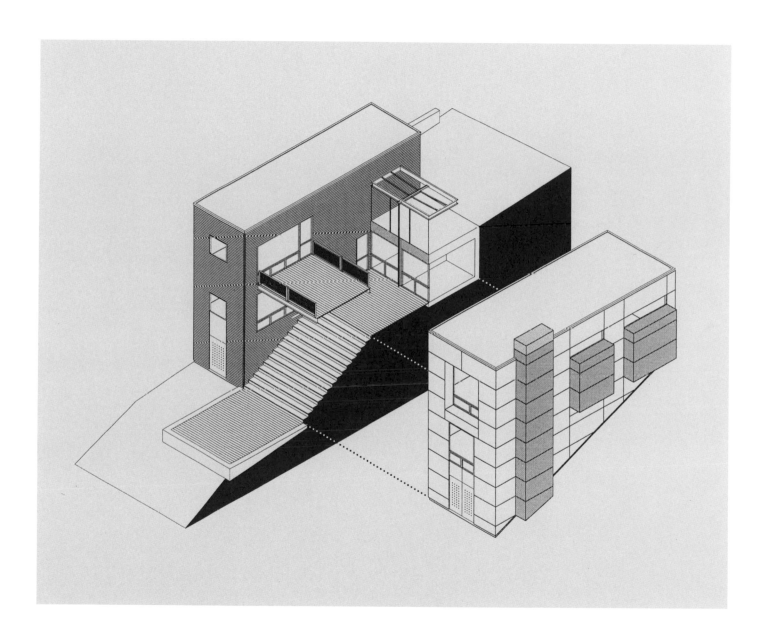

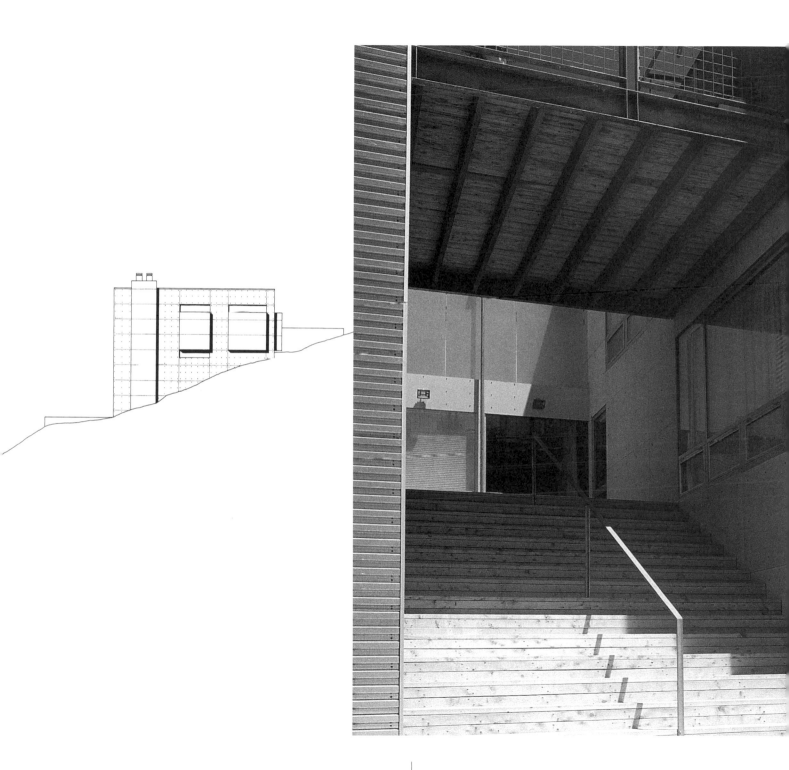

A glowing wall of translucent glass spans the area between the two volumes of the house. Together with a skylight held in place by a steel frame, this luminous wall defines the entrance to the house while also obscuring views to the interior courtyard from the street.

Large windows face onto the central courtyard; panoramic views of the surrounding area can be glimpsed through these windows, beyond the courtyard space. Smaller windows isolate discrete views of the adjacent hills and provide a sense of discovery as one moves through the house.

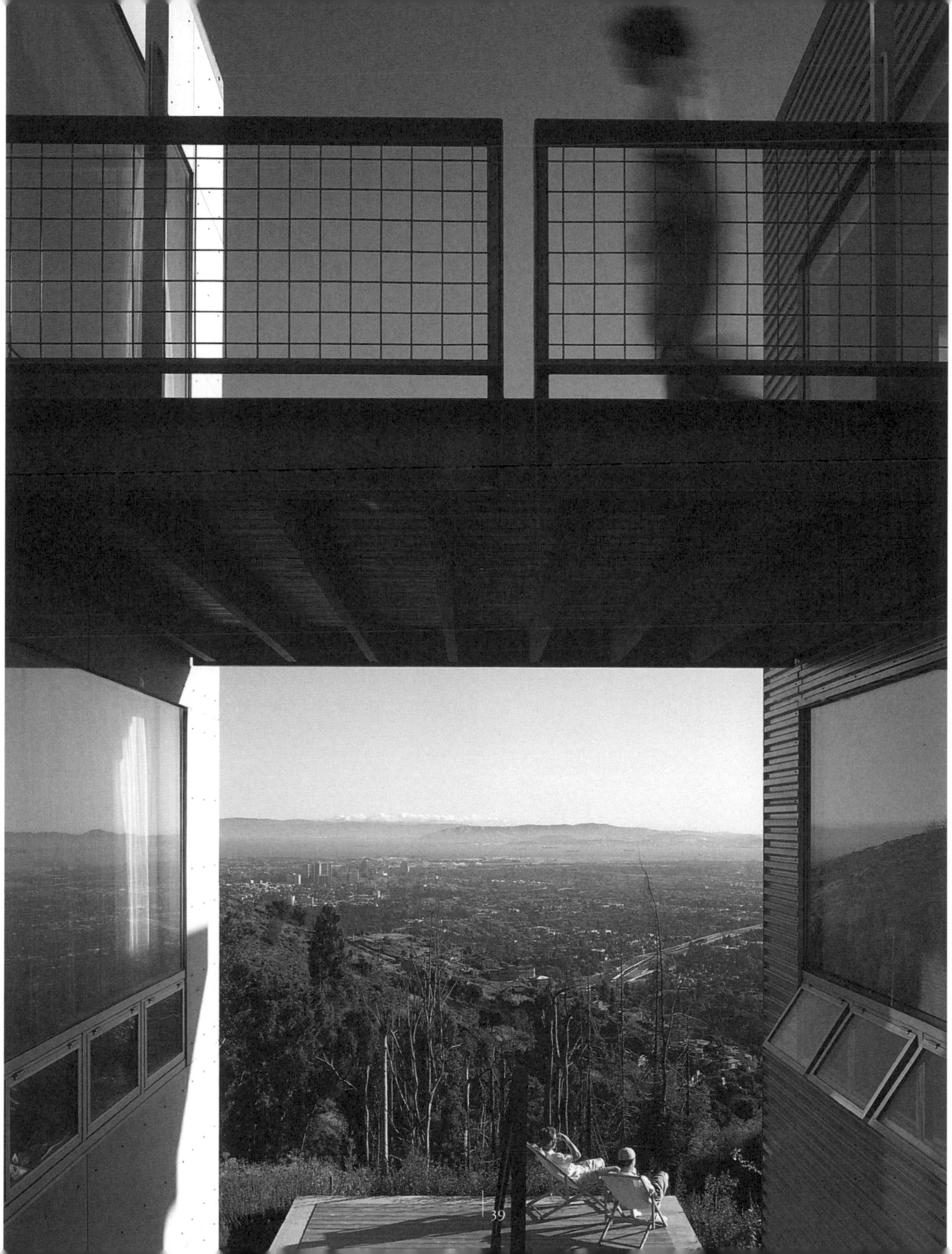

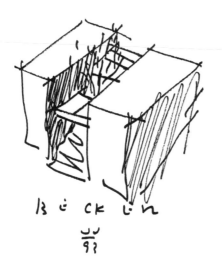

In order to emphasize the two distinct volumes of the house, the exterior is clad in two different materials—corrugated aluminum and cementboard panels. The dimensional relationships established within each volume are also different. These relationships are generated by the site and by the needs of the program.

GROUP ONE

This project occupies the southeast corner of an existing, poured-in-place concrete building in

San Francisco's South of Market district. The three-thousand square-foot space contains the

offices of a video production company engaged primarily in making television commercials.

As a reflection of the ephemeral nature of the client's business, all enclosing walls are

transparent and reflective. In addition, they are organized in a manner completely unrelated

to the geometry of the old warehouse; no wall is parallel or perpendicular to any other, nor to

G R O U P   O N E

the building, nor to the street grid of the neighborhood. The nature of the client's business is

further emphasized by contrasting the transparent, light-weight appearance of the glass walls

and floating ceiling plane to the heavy mass of the concrete structure that contains them. The

concrete is expressed much as it was found; the ceiling and mushroom columns have been

sandblasted and the floor, cleaned and sealed in the open work area. Black carpet is used in the

office spaces to create a jagged line of demarcation between heavy and light, the pre-existing

and the new, the permanent and the impermanent.

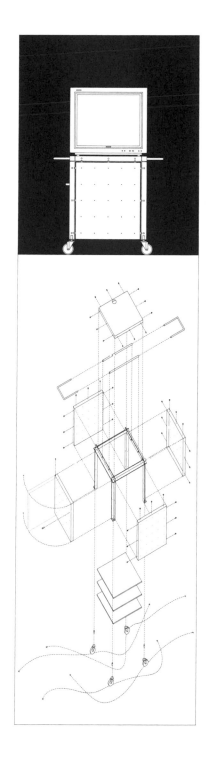

In that the principal activity of Group One is the production of television commercials, a cart was designed to hold a video monitor and other equipment. The cart, fabricated from steel and stainless steel, can be moved around the office and activated by remote control. It is meant to serve as an icon of the advertising media. Like the cart, desks, tables, credenzas, and book cases were also built according to architects' specifications. In light of budgetary constraints, all of the furniture was cut from plywood sheets in a manner designed to minimize waste.

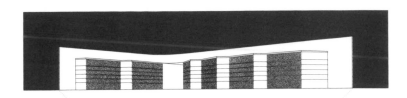

Conference space and offices are separated from the general work area by a long, multi-faceted glass wall. Individual panels of glass pivot to form office doors. Custom door handles were fabricated in steel.

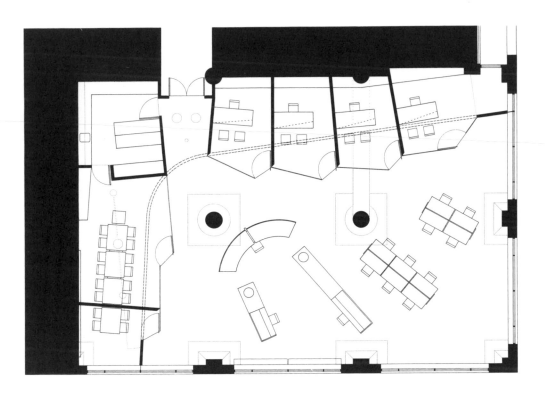

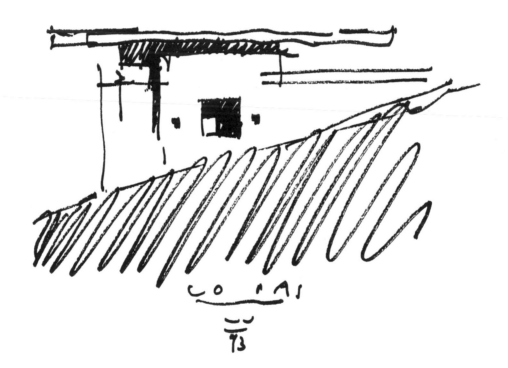

COLPAS

'93

This residence in Oakland, California, is organized under a thin, horizontal roof plane that hovers above the building's walls and extends out over a steep, downward-sloping hillside. A carport and entryway connect the house to the site on the uphill side. The main floor is arranged in an open plan and contains the kitchen and living areas. The lower level contains bedrooms and baths. The main volume of the house is compact. All of the walls are separated from the steel roof by a continuous band of glass; as a result, the plane of the roof appears to "float" above the building.

COPAS HOLLAND RESIDENCE

The living room is surrounded on three sides by frameless panels of glass. Uninterrupted by mullions, these large windows lend a feeling of openness to the room. The two steel beams of the roof are supported on eight steel columns, which pass up through the volume from ground level. The roof cantilevers twenty feet at each end, one end covering the living room and the other, providing shelter as a carport. A large balcony cantilevers away from the building to the south. Two glass doors link the balcony to the house and allow for the continuous movement from inside to outside and back again.

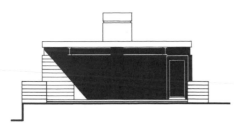

In order to emphasize the solidity of its form and its connection to the ground, the base of the house receives minimal glazing. Custom milled wood boards applied to the exterior provide texture and relief; the pattern of repeating horizontal lines they create mirrors the form of the roof, a "floating" horizontal plane that cantilevers twenty feet at either end.

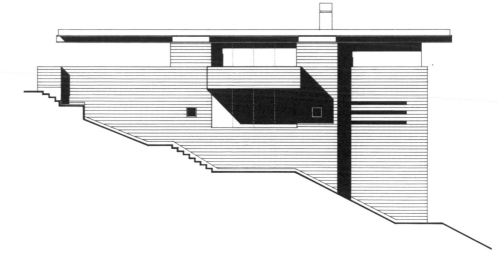

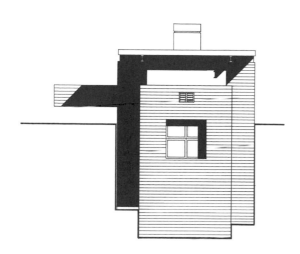

Steel columns embedded within the center of the building support two steel beams seventy feet in length; these beams, in turn, support a steel roof deck above. The walls of the building are separated from the roof by sheets of glass set into aluminum channels. In the case of an earthquake, these channels allow the structure to move without breaking the glass.

Frameless panels of glass give the
appearance that the roof hovers above
the floor without the support of walls.
Views to the surrounding landscape
remain completely unobstructed.
Throughout the house, floors made
of polished concrete contain hot water
tubing that provides radiant heat.

Located at the end of an alleyway south of Market Street in San Francisco, this space houses the office of Jim Jennings Architecture. Inserted into an existing structure from the 1930s, the studio space is experimental: architectural elements are designed for use in the studio, manufactured off-site and configured within the space. Doors, tables, a conference room, "light slots" in the ceiling, and scrims of galvanized steel, glass, plywood, and clear anodized aluminum take their form from the standard dimensions and fabrication requirements of the materials used. The

25 BRUSH PLACE

standard dimension of one-eight-inch thick aluminum panels, for instance, determined the diameter of the conference room. The structural limitations of the aluminum skin make an outer frame necessary. The interior panels, together with the exterior skeleton, in the end create a very rigid structure. This project also explores the belief that materials have a tactile quality often at odds with one's perception of them. The visual softness of aluminum, for example, contradicts the common perception of metal as a hard material. This project affords the opportunity to investigate these conflicting sensory experiences in greater detail.

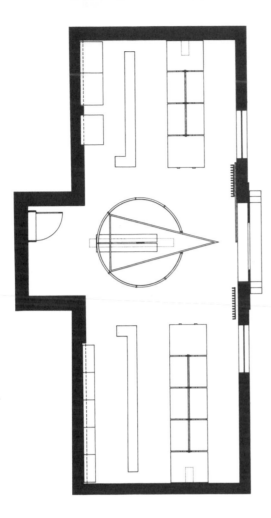

The entrance to the studio is made of
sliding panels of galvanized steel and
sandblasted glass. A conference room
fabricated in clear anodized aluminum
occupies the center of the space. The
conference room takes the name of "kiva"
after the cylindrical, subterranean rooms
within which the Anasazi Indians took
care of community business. Like other
elements within the studio, the conference
room is designed to be disassembled
and reassembled in a different location.

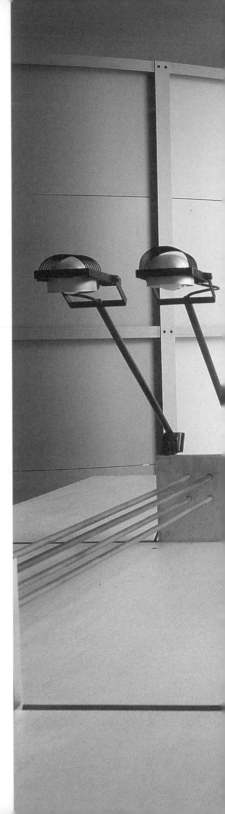

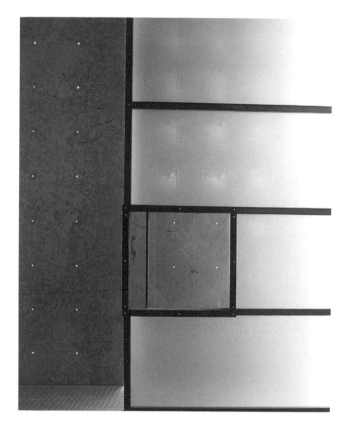

In making an environment for his own use and occupation, the architect felt compelled to experiment. Doors, tables, light fixtures, and window scrims are designed and fabricated for use within the space.

A low voltage aluminum lamp uses perforated sheets of metal and machined parts in its construction. All materials used as screens or walls are designed to provide varying degrees of visual separation. Thin slits between solid panels of aluminum, translucent and clear glass, and perforated sheets of galvanized steel are juxtaposed in ways that control the passage of light, provide limited views, and create privacy.

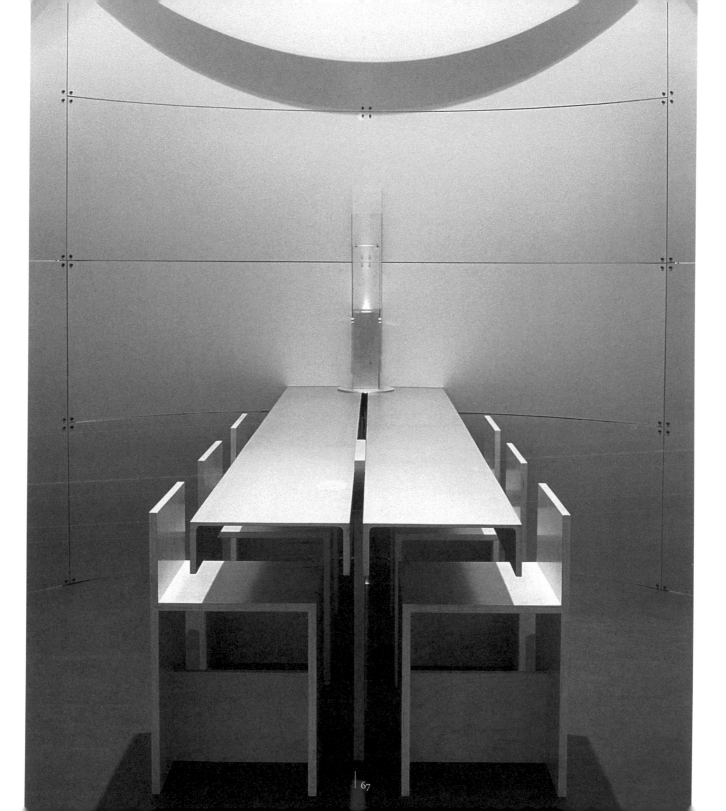

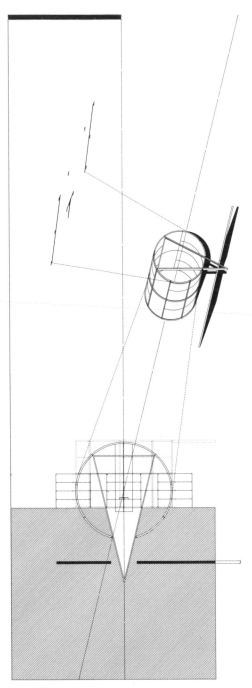

The kiva, shown in plan, section and elevation

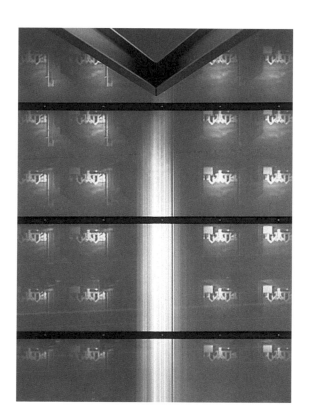

One enters the studio through two ten-foot square sliding panels—one of galvanized steel and one of translucent sandblasted glass. When the steel panel was fabricated, a grid of very small holes was drilled through the plate. During daylight hours, each of these holes acts as a *camera obscura*, projecting an image of the exterior alleyway onto the translucent glass of the second sliding panel. These images are visible—although inverted—from the interior of the studio.

This project for a cemetery master plan in Colma, California, is designed to occupy a site constrained by the Bay Area Rapid Transit extension to the San Francisco airport on one side and by a major road on the other. The clients of the Italian Cemetery wanted to recall a tradition of memorial architecture that stems from Roman times. The cemetery is comprised of a series of distinct funerary forms connected by a path. One enters the monument near the midpoint of the path, into a large courtyard or piazza. From there, one either ascends toward a tower located at one

ITALIAN CEMETERY

end, from which one can look out over the rest of the cemetery, or descends toward a mausoleum located at the opposite end, into a submerged courtyard filled with water. Placed along the processional path are a number of memorial spaces: catacombs, the piazza, a hypostyle hall, a columbarium, and family tombs. These spaces provide places of repose and contemplation along the processional route. Experienced together, the spaces of the cemetery reinforce a connection between motion and stasis, between the living and the dead, between the temporal and the eternal.

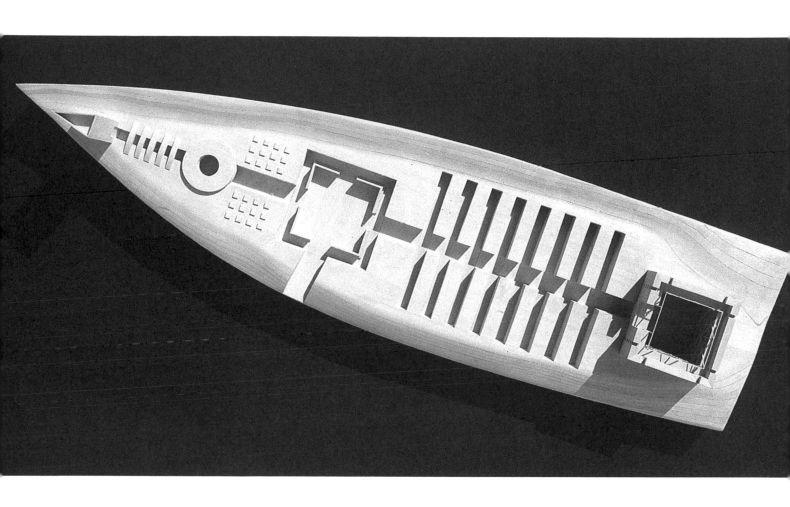

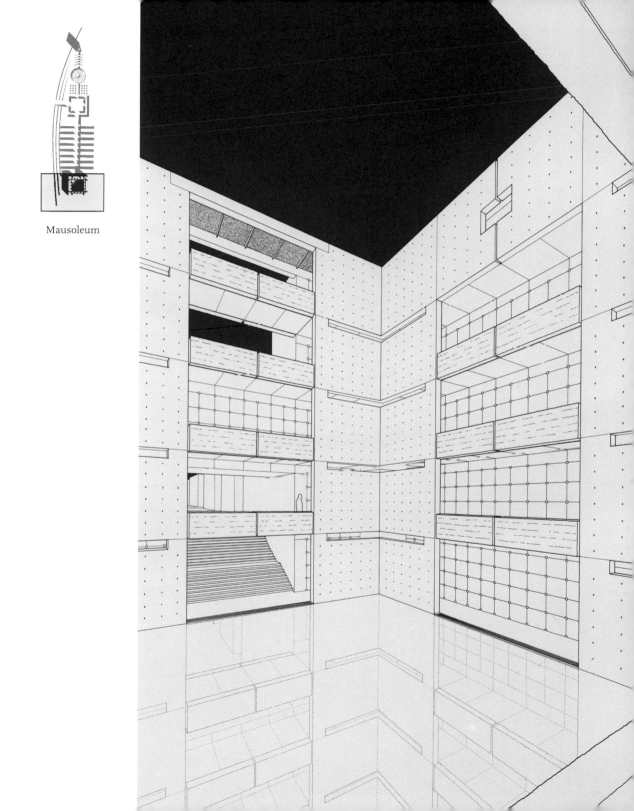

Mausoleum

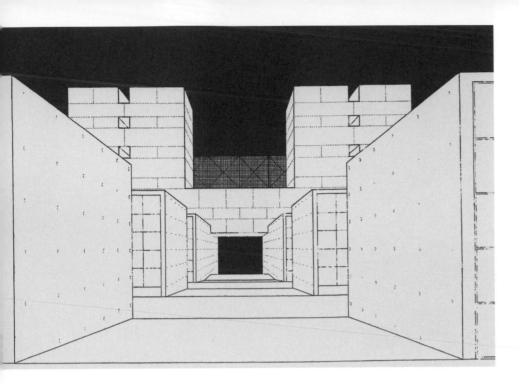

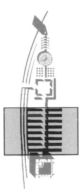

Catacombs

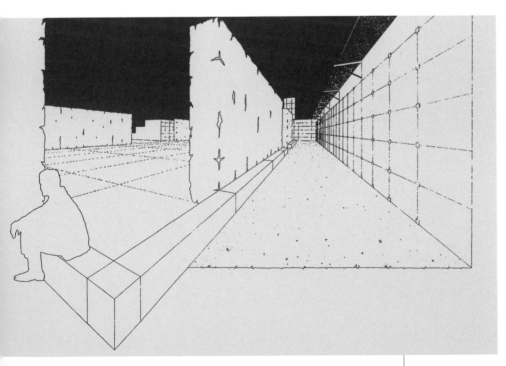

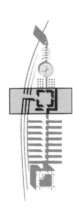

Piazza

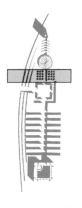

Hypostyle Hall

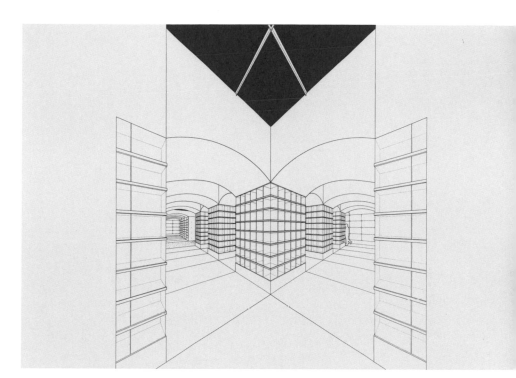

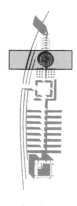

Columbarium

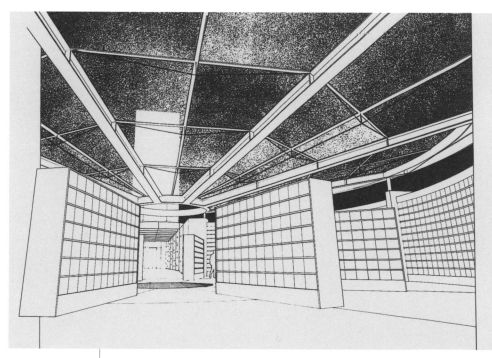

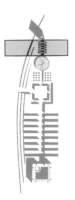

Family Tombs

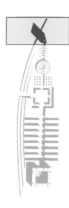

Memorial Tower

"It was this eternal progression and eternal recurrence, the sublimation of an eternal wandering, that was given form..."

Sigfried Gideon
The Beginnings of Architecture

"When we come to a mound in the wood, six feet long and three feet wide, raised to a pyramidal form by means of a spade, we become serious and something in us says: somebody lies here. This is architecture."

Adolf Loos
Architecture

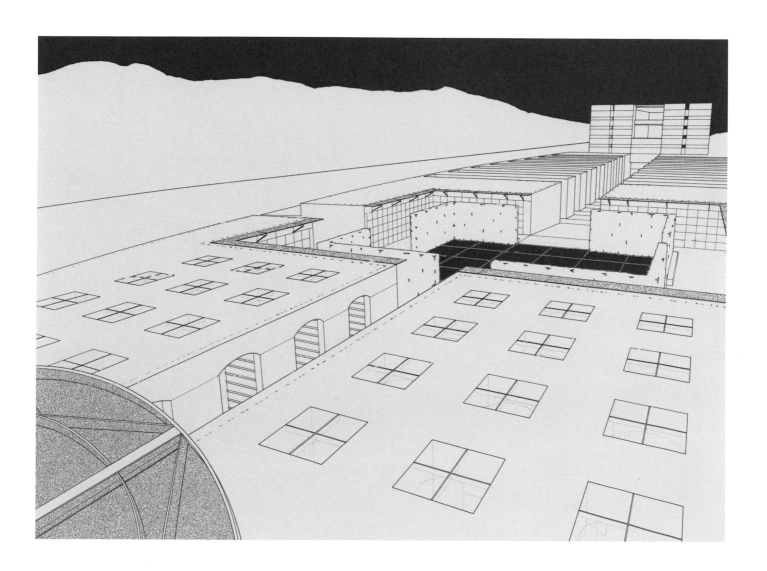

The site for this project is located on the edge of a fourteen-acre parcel of rolling grassland in Calistoga,

California, covered with live oaks, madrones, and other native vegetation. A weekend residence com-

missioned by two professionals who live in San Francisco during the week, the house was designed to

be easily maintained and to allow the owners to "open and close" the building with minimal effort.

Both the long, narrow shape of the building and its north-south orientation facilitate cross-ventilation by

GANDIA STEPHENSON RESIDENCE

taking advantage of the prevailing westerly breeze. The simple gable-roofed structure is also shaped and

sited to preserve a generous portion of level ground for outdoor living. The building opens onto a terrace

to the west and a large gravel courtyard to the east through two adjacent banks of french doors. The

courtyard, surrounded by a wisteria-covered wood trellis, serves as an extension of the living and dining

area inside. The exterior of the house is clad in corrugated metal, chosen for its compatibility with the

rural environment of Sonoma County.

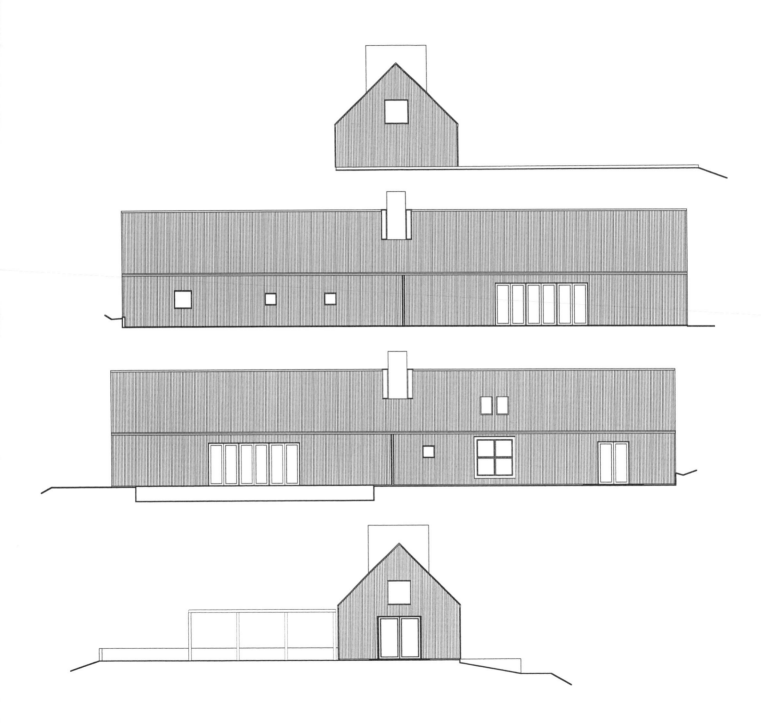

Like the exterior, the interior of the building is clad in galvanized steel. Standard open web steel joists hold up ribbed steel decking. Stainless steel cables—usually used as standing rigging on sailboats—tie the roof trusses together.

Located on San Francisco's Telegraph Hill, this building was designed in an attempt to make livable spaces within the constraints of a dense urban environment. A large house and two small apartments have privacy, access to views, and multiple connections to outside areas: on each level of the building, one may open a door and step outside onto a protected courtyard, balcony, or terrace. The terrace located at the very top of the building commands a 360 degree view of the city and the bay. Parking is contained in a subterranean garage located below the main entry courtyard. Pedestrians enter this courtyard through a gate at the sidewalk made of stainless steel and translucent glass. A landscaped path leads past a pool containing water plants and down a broad flight of stairs. From

OLIVER RESIDENCE

the courtyard, one steps into a forty-foot high space, part of a concrete cylinder that occupies the center of the building. This cylinder—twenty-two feet wide and made of white poured-in-place concrete—contains the circulation elements for the main house: stairs, bridges, and an elevator. The bridges and roof of the cylinder are made of steel and sandblasted glass. Light that penetrates these elements is reflected off the elevator shaft, clad in clear anodized aluminum panels. In contrast to the cylinder, the living areas of the main house are constructed in materials more commonly associated with domestic architecture; these areas have maple floors, neutral ceilings, and expansive wall planes designed to display an extensive collection of contemporary art.

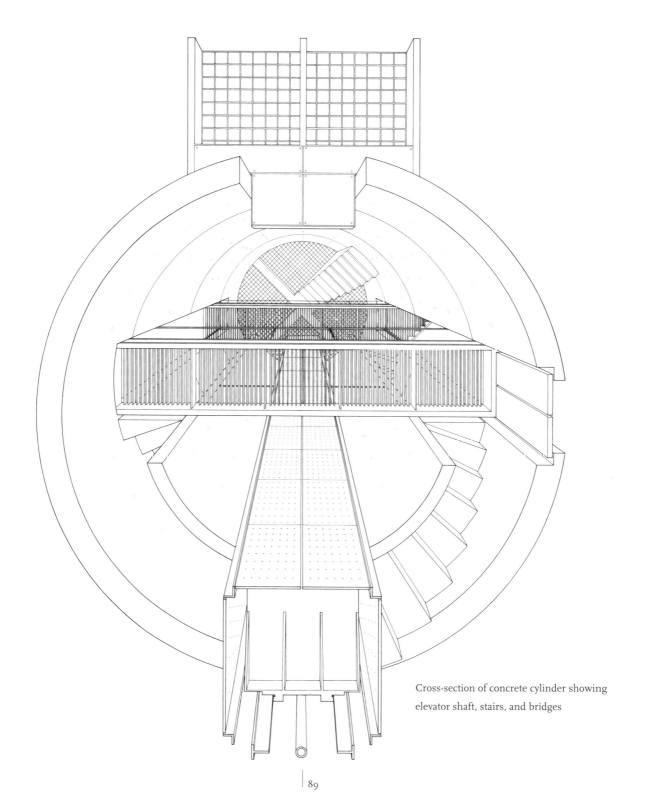

Cross-section of concrete cylinder showing
elevator shaft, stairs, and bridges

The T-shaped site slopes downward toward the bay. A series of terraced gardens are placed on axis with the concrete cylinder that occupies the center of the building.

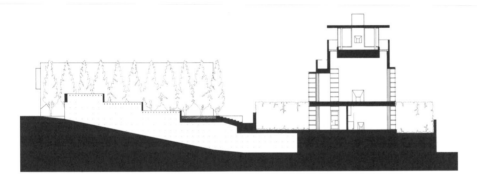

This axis sets up a perceived symmetry—one that is superceded by the asymmetrical arrangement of spaces on both the interior and exterior of the building.

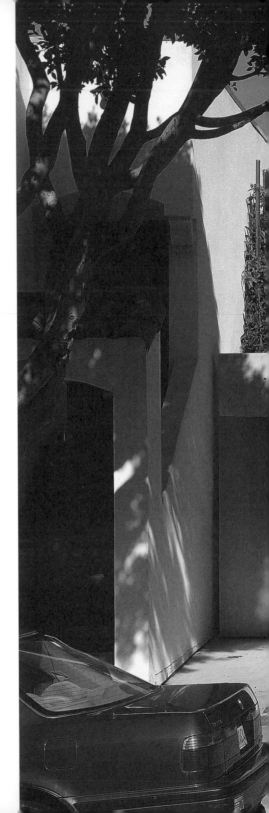

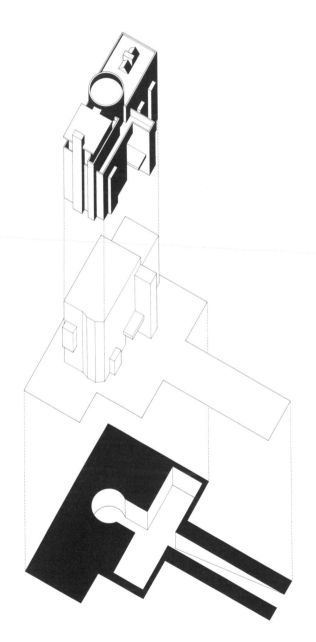

The building appears to sit on the site as an object in a garden; in actuality, it is an intricate set of vertically layered spaces, divided into three residential units. These units are linked through the circulation system contained within the cylinder. Spaces vary in volume and in the character of light that enters them through exterior windows and the central skylight.

Two steel and glass bridges laterally traverse the concrete cylinder at the center of the house and connect various living areas to one another. Moving through the building from ground level toward the roof, one moves from dark to light, from containment to expansiveness, from voluminous height to an intense awareness of the horizon, framed by the roof slab that caps the building.

This house in northern California was designed for a couple with grown children. Because the site is ringed with trees, the house is sited in a clearing located at the center. The house is formed by two long, intersecting bars that divide the site into four unequal quadrants. Each quadrant contains a programmatic function that relates to the function contained in adjacent spaces within the house. The quadrant located next to the garages and entry door serves as an entry court. Two quadrants containing sculpture are situated next to the living areas of the house. The fourth quadrant is occupied by a garden and is located adjacent to the kitchen and informal living area.

PRIVATE RESIDENCE

One wing of the house is made of poured-in-place concrete; the other wing, of cement plaster. The concrete wing contains the social functions of the house: dining, living, and guest rooms. The plaster wing contains family functions: bedrooms, baths, kitchen, and informal living areas. A two-story gallery is located at the intersection of the two wings. The gallery, illuminated by several long, narrow skylights, is designed to display a portion of the clients' collection of contemporary art. Each of the building's two wings terminates at one end in a large terrace. Covered by a vaulted, copper-clad roof, the concrete wing ends in a terrace that faces east toward San Francisco Bay. The plaster wing extends to the south and supports a sixty-foot long pool framed by a clearing in the trees.

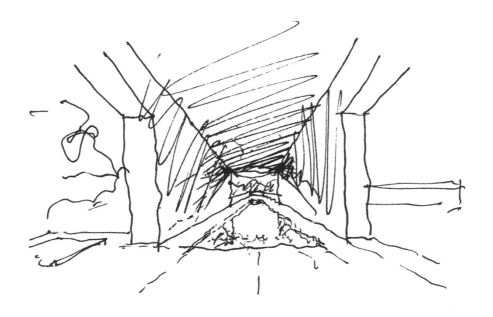

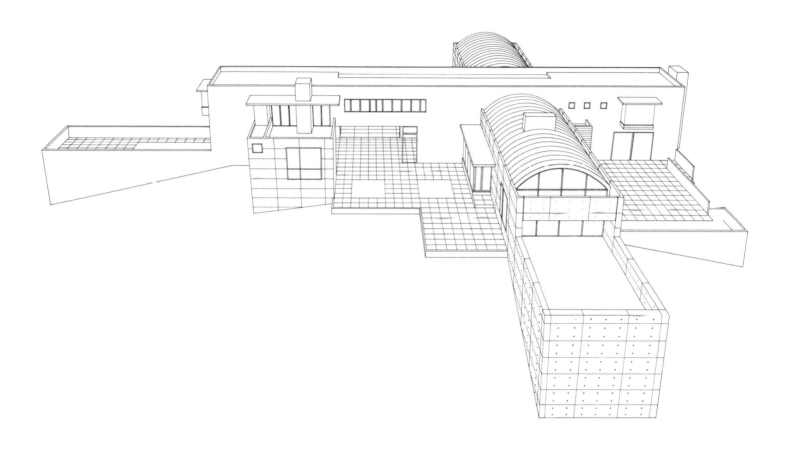

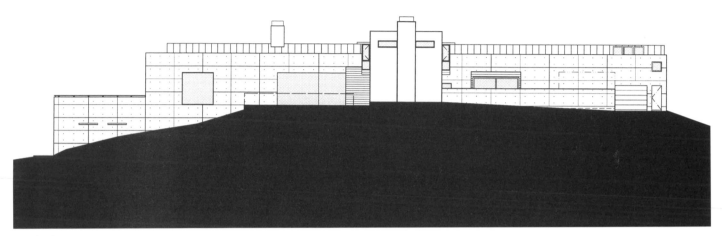

North elevation

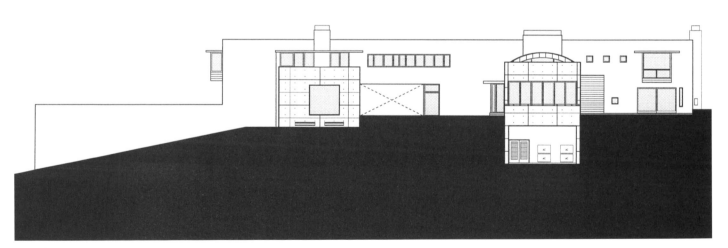

East elevation

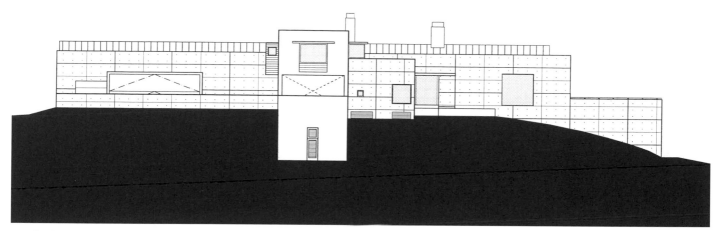

South elevation

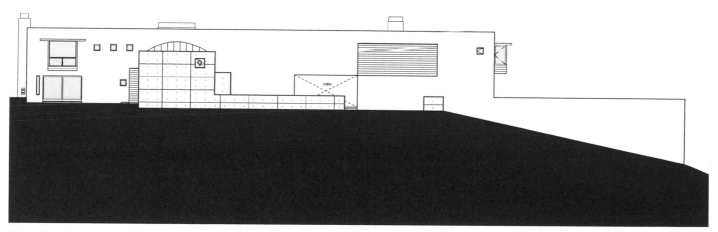

West elevation

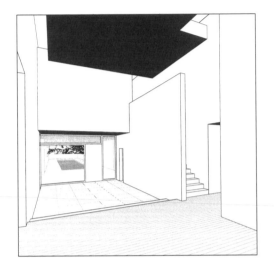
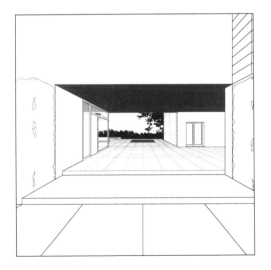

The painter Giorgio Morandi writes, "I am especially a painter of the kind of still life composition that communicates a sense of tranquillity and privacy, moods which I have always valued above all else." Morandi nourishes a poetic resonance in the small. A continuity approaching the timeless is intrinsic to his work. The volume and lines in his compositions are "frankly modern" without polemics. The various life circumstances that limited his production did not reduce the rigorous measurements of space he forged in his tiny Bologna studio. An affinity between architectural form and the bottles and bowls in a Morandi still life might be found in the way that repetition erodes identity. Like the basic volumes of architecture, these household goods are always reduced.

Thinking of Morandi as a collateral model for an architect brings up several questions. What is an architecture without artifice? Without dilettantism? When is an architecture real and ideal and at once modern and classic? The most measured abstract compositions seem to provoke these

EPISTEMOLOGICAL OBSTACLES

questions. In thinking about the origin and limits of knowledge (i.e., the epistemology) of architecture, the minimal stands as an obstacle—the silence of the sublime blocking the noise of the baroque. What seems at first an obstacle finally provides a bridge for thought. As in a Zen statement, paradox is essential.

For some artists, like the painter Agnes Martin, the epistemological emerges in formal absence. She writes, "my paintings have neither objects nor space nor time, nor anything—no forms." Martin's aspiration approaches the limits of what can be known about art; she walks over the horizon into the 'desert' of pure emptiness staked out by Kazimir Malevich eighty years earlier.

Like Morandi and Martin, Jennings focuses on the small and records the known in a sensitive sparseness. Attention to light, shadow, and texture constitutes a major ingredient of his work. The framework of this book—the choice of one project equalling one year—parallels the measured balance of his approach. Incised in the cardboard cover of Jennings' book, 10/10, the two sparse numbers with the digital 1, 0, 1, 0 are analogous to the amplification of the minimal in Jennings' work, the geometric intensity of simple rectangles, the range of color in black and white . . .

A horizon of emptiness and silence is the focus of Jim Jennings' project for the Visiting Artists Suites in Geyserville, California. The artists' chambers are formed between ruthlessly simple cross-walls slicing through a hill. The heart of the section, with its subtle shifts, is termed a "perceptual telescope." Perspective phenomena—the elongation and foreshortening of space—generates this double house. The architecture is focused on the space beyond what is contained within the architectural object itself, a space beyond the horizon's oceanic emptiness.

In Jennings' project for the Italian Cemetery in San Francisco, a partially realized project which is for the architect very real, he compares the origins of the cemetery with the origins of architecture. Questions of mass and void, the temporal and the eternal, the limited and the limitless, haunt this

STEVEN HOLL

work. Here it seems, Jennings' thought-experiment has a transparent object at its center. The form of the plan—an eternally-drifting ship—collects elements to which Jennings continually returns. A concave glass roof placed within the glass cylinder collects water in a cycle of evaporation, collection, and return to earth that stands as a phenomenon parallel that still time of pure geometry. With timelessness, however, comes the nullity embodied in nonexistence. The Italian Cemetery project characterizes Jennings' philosophy in what he describes as "between the living and the dead, between motion and stasis."

The Oliver House on Telegraph Hill embodies the minimalist cause completely, from landscape to space to art. Wonderful works by Agnes Martin, Richard Serra, Robert Mangold, and Sol Lewitt bring the stillness of the interiors to life. Opening the translucent glass street gate during an August sunset reveals a surprisingly vast stone court with transverse strips of green ground cover, mottled in sunlight. Entering the cylindrical center, one walks on sandblasted glass treads that allow light to vibrate on the smooth, white concrete walls. From room to room, the glass bridges the cylinder space, back and forth in a more fluid way than suggested by the plan. Pausing on the bridge one sees a beautiful, subtle, floating, red thread rectangle by the artist Fred Sandback. As in a Morandi still life, the object becomes an epistemological obstacle, aspiring to peace and a marvelous timelessness.

PROJECT NOTES

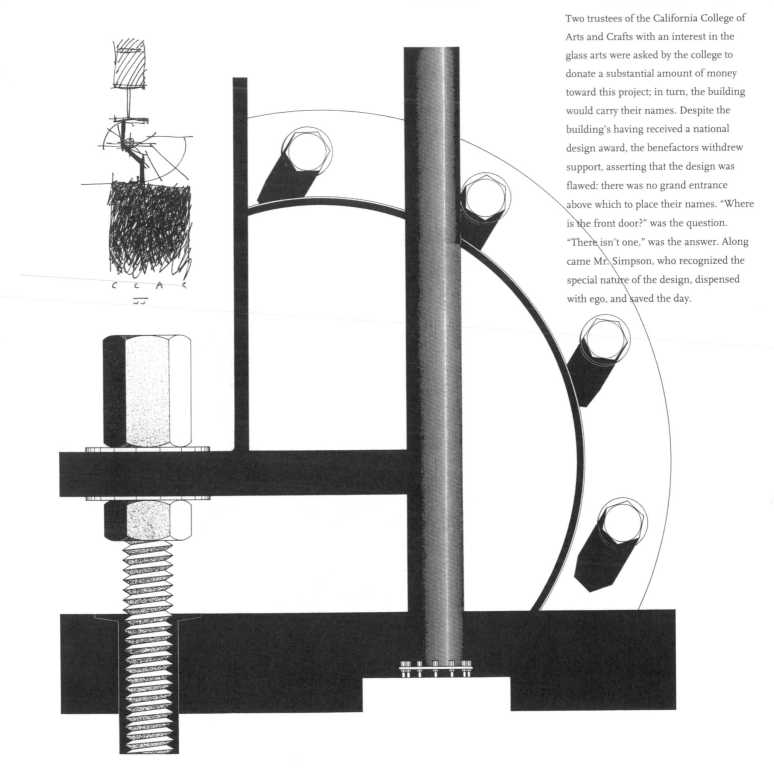

Two trustees of the California College of Arts and Crafts with an interest in the glass arts were asked by the college to donate a substantial amount of money toward this project; in turn, the building would carry their names. Despite the building's having received a national design award, the benefactors withdrew support, asserting that the design was flawed: there was no grand entrance above which to place their names. "Where is the front door?" was the question. "There isn't one," was the answer. Along came Mr. Simpson, who recognized the special nature of the design, dispensed with ego, and saved the day.

BARCLAY SIMPSON SCULPTURE STUDIO

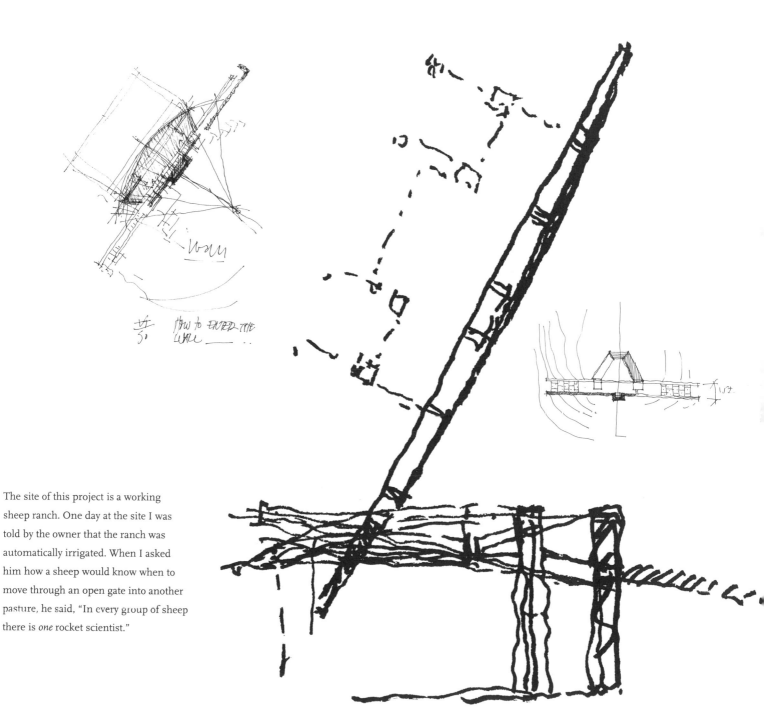

How to enter the wall ...

The site of this project is a working sheep ranch. One day at the site I was told by the owner that the ranch was automatically irrigated. When I asked him how a sheep would know when to move through an open gate into another pasture, he said, "In every group of sheep there is *one* rocket scientist."

VISITING ARTIST SUITES

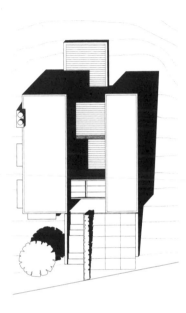

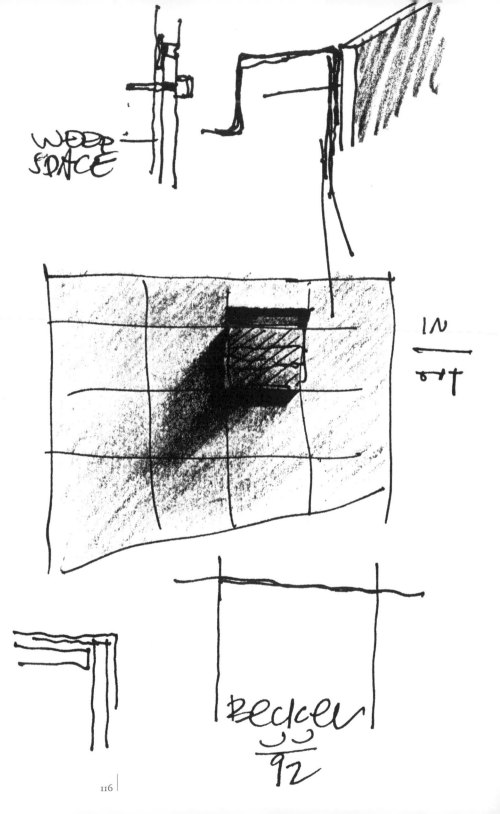

WOOD SPACE

BECKER 92

One afternoon when the Becker house was nearing completion, I was standing in the road taking photographs of the front of the building. A car approached slowly, pulled over to the side of the road, and parked near where I stood. The driver emerged and walked toward me. "Are you the owner of this house?" he asked. "No, I'm the architect." "Well," he said, "I'm having a hell of a time getting approval for a house down the street, so I'm going to take a picture of this house to show them downtown. If they allowed this thing, they should approve *anything*!"

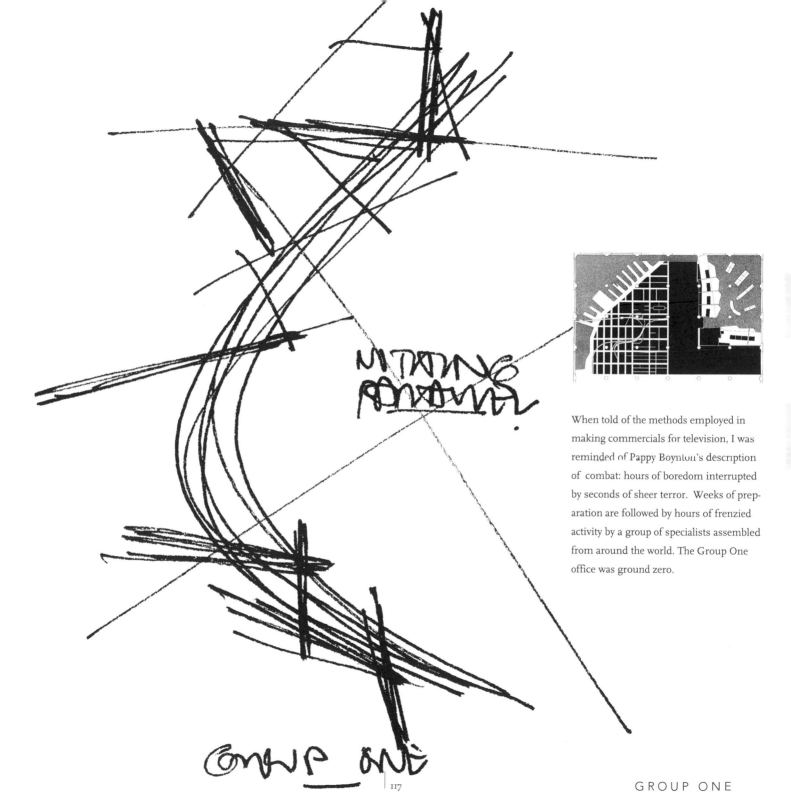

When told of the methods employed in making commercials for television, I was reminded of Pappy Boynton's description of combat: hours of boredom interrupted by seconds of sheer terror. Weeks of preparation are followed by hours of frenzied activity by a group of specialists assembled from around the world. The Group One office was ground zero.

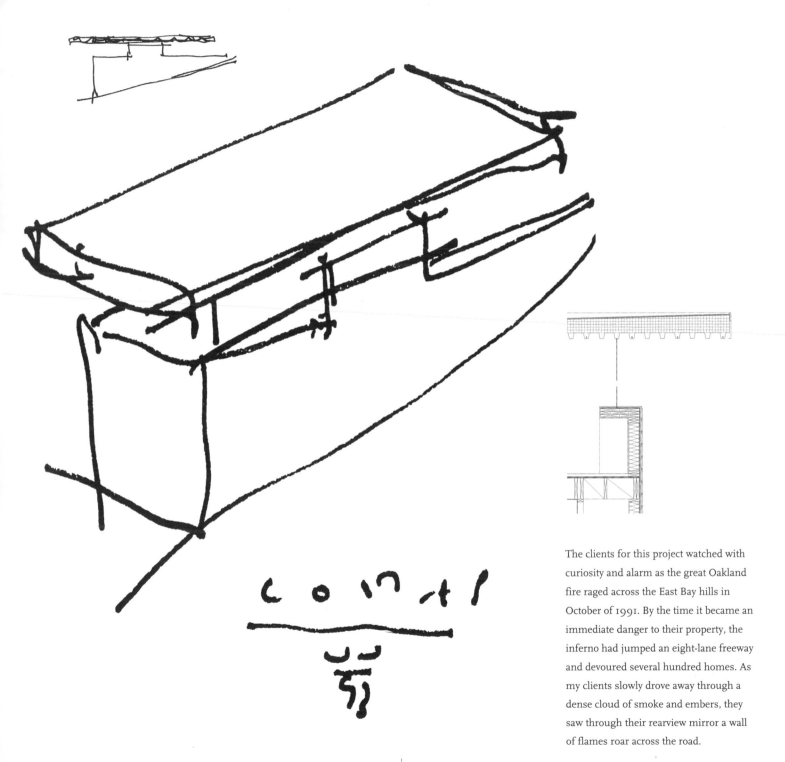

The clients for this project watched with curiosity and alarm as the great Oakland fire raged across the East Bay hills in October of 1991. By the time it became an immediate danger to their property, the inferno had jumped an eight-lane freeway and devoured several hundred homes. As my clients slowly drove away through a dense cloud of smoke and embers, they saw through their rearview mirror a wall of flames roar across the road.

All of the elements contained in this project—
table tops, undercarriage structures, shutters,
chairs, and conference room—are shaped by
the size and characteristics of the materials
used. The cylindrical "kiva," for instance,
evolved in much the same way as the original
architecture upon which it was based; the
dimensions of the materials used (in this case,
aluminum panels rather than mud bricks)
determined the diameter of the room.

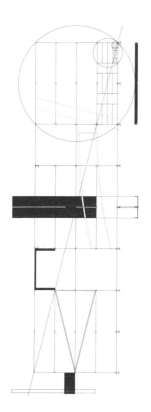

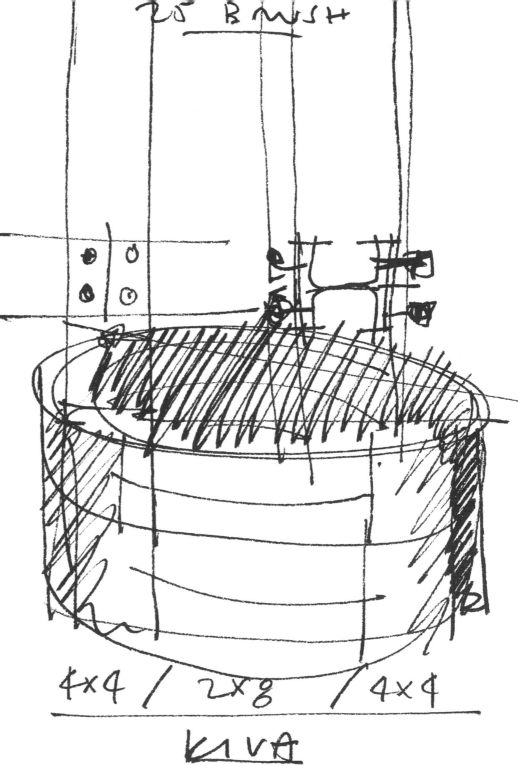

25 BRUSH

4x4 / 2x8 / 4x4

KIVA

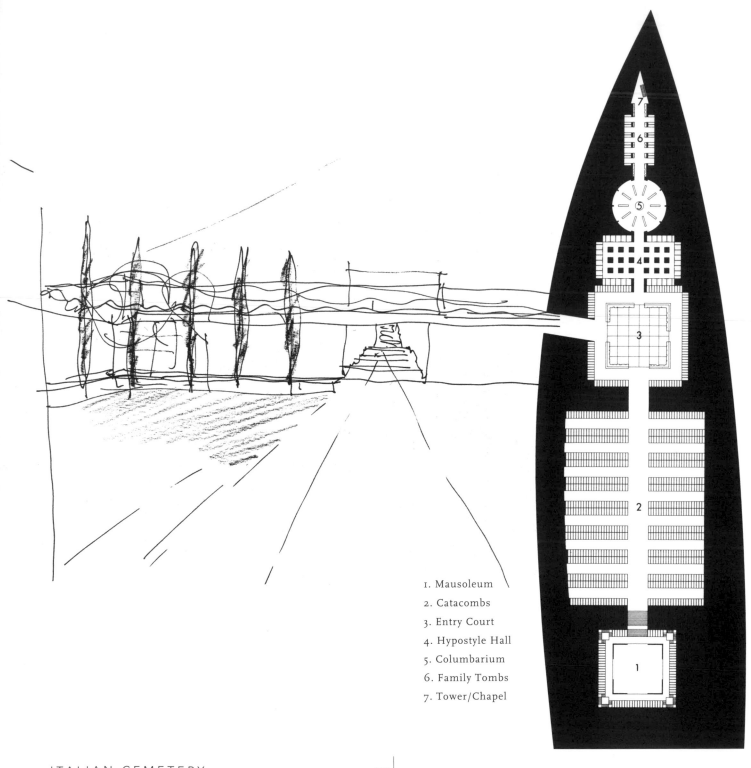

1. Mausoleum
2. Catacombs
3. Entry Court
4. Hypostyle Hall
5. Columbarium
6. Family Tombs
7. Tower/Chapel

ITALIAN CEMETERY

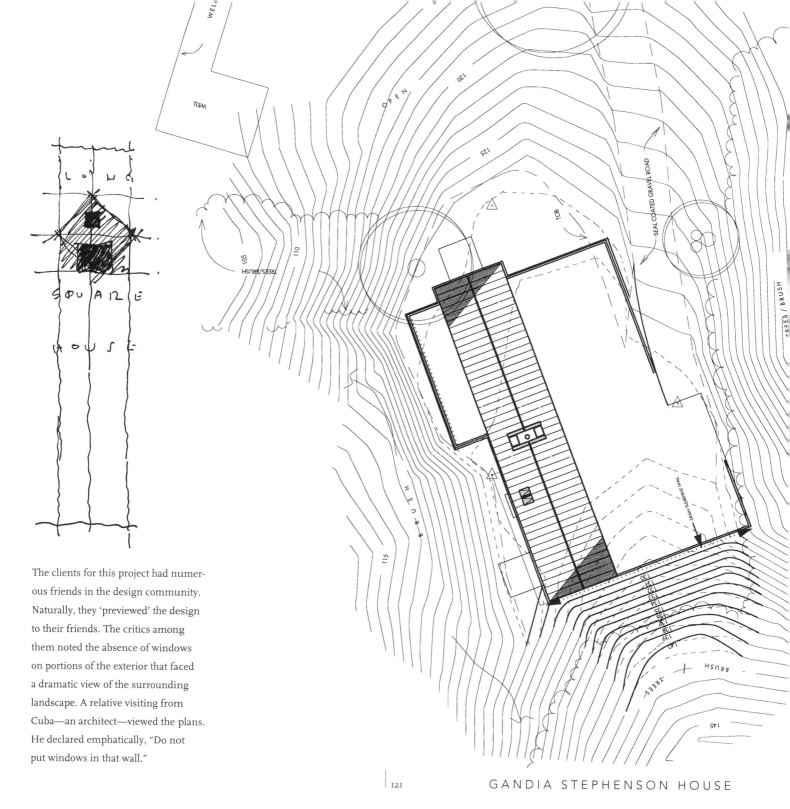

The clients for this project had numerous friends in the design community. Naturally, they 'previewed' the design to their friends. The critics among them noted the absence of windows on portions of the exterior that faced a dramatic view of the surrounding landscape. A relative visiting from Cuba—an architect—viewed the plans. He declared emphatically, "Do not put windows in that wall."

GANDIA STEPHENSON HOUSE

Two adjacent neighbors aggressively
objected to this project during the
approval process. When construction
began, one of them called 911.

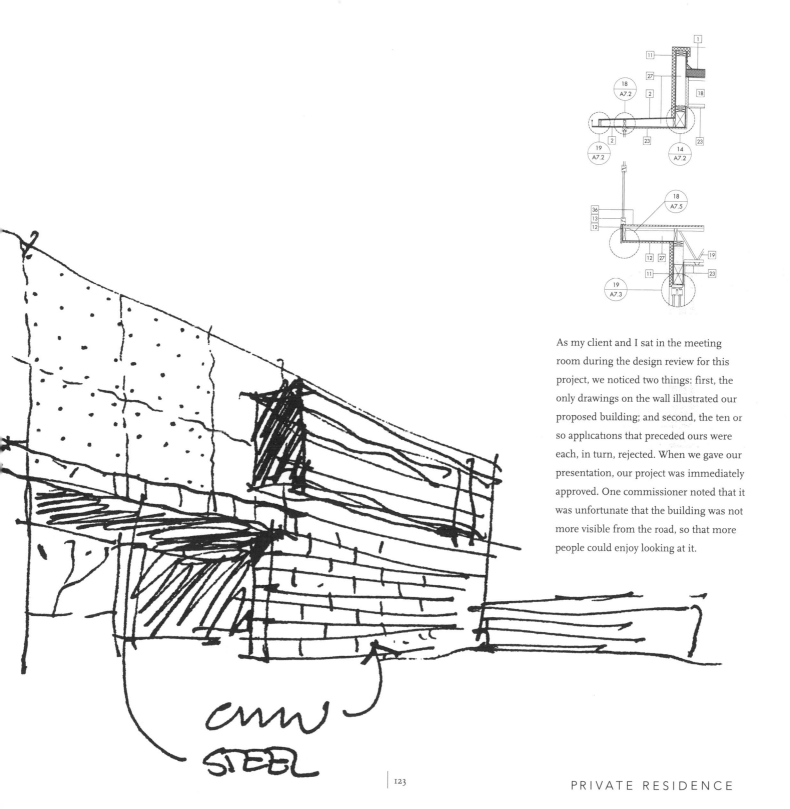

As my client and I sat in the meeting room during the design review for this project, we noticed two things: first, the only drawings on the wall illustrated our proposed building; and second, the ten or so applications that preceded ours were each, in turn, rejected. When we gave our presentation, our project was immediately approved. One commissioner noted that it was unfortunate that the building was not more visible from the road, so that more people could enjoy looking at it.

STEEL

STEEL

PRIVATE RESIDENCE

PUBLISHER'S ACKNOWLEDGMENTS

This, the second monograph in a series of books devoted to the work of West Coast architects, focuses on ten interesting and varied commissions by Jim Jennings. The sketches, developmental drawings, photographs, and comments presented herein give insight into Jim's work and into the process he uses to design.

Throughout our long friendship, I have always admired Jim's precise eye. Both through the camera lens, in his wonderful photographs, and with his hand, in his clear drawings, his ability to analyze and to communicate in a constructive manner throughout the entire building process is evident. I've often seen Jim take a rough sketch done in the field, dimension it, give it to a craftsman, and get it built without another thought.

My first contacts with Jim were in the 1970s, as young architects working in various offices in the San Francisco Bay area. What I remember most about those times is the excitement we got out of sharing inspirational moments. Photographs, books on poetry and music, and unique architecture and architects provided very important stimuli. Our own photographs, usually of abstracted landscapes, rural buildings, and objects from California always became the subject of conversation. We shared an idealistic impression of what architecture could be.

Three strong images from this early period stand out in my mind: Jim sharing his record collection of the California composer Harry Partch; him standing with Luis Barragan at the architect's famous house in Mexico City; and us reading Aldo Rossi's *Architecture of the City* while traveling through the Mexican desert in a Volkswagen van. We both have a love of and an appreciation for the calmness of the desert, its abstract beauty, and its harsh light. We were architectural partners for many years before our lives took different directions; looking over his work from the past ten years, it is clear that Jim has remained true to his architectural ambitions and dreams. It's an honor to share his work with a larger audience.

A wonderful collaboration has occurred with the creation of this monograph. Michael Cronan and his assistant Joseph Stitzlein, working with Jim's office, came up with the original graphic design concept. Our design staff of Sandra Shuhert and John Clifford coordinated the final graphics, and Nancy Eklund provided editorial direction. Jim's design staff, including Cheri Fraser and Erik Tellander, produced additional drawings for some of the projects, as did Dean Orr.

Special thanks goes to Pilar Viladas and Steven Holl for providing the text that brackets the projects. Our interlocking friendships over the years have made their contributions very special.

William K. Stout, Publisher

Jim Jennings would like to acknowledge the exceptional work of the following individuals:

Amy Adamson, Kevin Batcho, Russ Beaudin, Lilian Chan, Vincent Chew, Michael Cobb, John DeForest, Alfonso Fabrega, John Fatzinger, Cheri Fraser, Christina Gearin, John Holmes, Thomas Holzmueller, Alexander Homs, Andy Jennings, Mark Jensen, Jay Kammen, Emma Kim, Antonio Lau, Andrew Lee, Michael Lee, Lina Levan, Karen Linnsen, Lee Loomis, Chris Manwaring, Elizabeth Manwaring, Mary Herder McFarland, David Milner, Thomas Müller, Carlos Navarrette, Pauline Pattajoti, Tim Perks, Anthony Poon, Whitney Sander, Bruno Sarret, Brit Schlinke, Craig Steely, Charlie Stott, May Sung, Les Taylor, Erik Tellander, Russell Thomsen, Melina Visone, and Christopher Weir.

PHOTOGRAPHERS' CREDITS

Richard Barnes, San Francisco, CA, 36, 37, 38, 39, 40, 41, 43, 91, 93, 95 (left, right), 96, 97, 98, 99, 100

Reiner Blunck, Hirschau, Germany, 55, 56, 57, 58, 59

Benny Chan, Santa Monica, CA, 127

John Clifford, San Francisco, CA, 102

Frank Davison, San Francisco, CA, 20, 80, 82-83, 85, 86, 87

Christopher Irion, San Francisco, CA, 44-45, 48, 49, 51

Jim Jennings Architecture, San Francisco, CA, 91, 94 (left, right)

Joel Puliatti, San Francisco, CA, 22-23

Alan Weintraub, San Francisco, CA, 11, 16, 17, 18, 19, 21, 31, 32, 61, 62-63, 64, 65, 66, 67, 69

Italian Cemetery, Courtyard Mausoleum, Colma, California

10

10